The waving sheep

Story by Beverley Randell

Illustrated by Linda McClelland

"Look, the rain has stopped," said Jessica. "Let's go outside."

"See if you can find some flowers," said Grandma. "You can walk over the hill to the back of the farm. Let's put your boots on, Daniel."

The children walked up the hill.

Jessica waved at Dad, who was bringing the cows in for milking.

At the top of the hill Daniel said,
"I can see a sheep waving."

"Sheep don't wave," said Jessica.

But the sheep waved again.
It waved all its legs.

"It can't get up," said Jessica.
"Come on — let's go
and help it."

Jessica and Daniel
pushed and pushed, but
the rain had made the sheep's wool
very wet and heavy.
"We can't do it," said Jessica.
"Dad is milking the cows.
He can't come to help us.
I'll go and get Grandma."

Jessica ran all the way home
to tell Grandma.
"Where's the sheep?" she said.

"Up by the top fence," said Jessica.
"Come on. I can show you."
Grandma rode up the hill
on the farm bike.

Jessica, Daniel, and Grandma tried to help the sheep. They pushed, and pushed, and pushed some more.

The sheep rolled over. Then they helped it get up.

"Don't let it go, yet," said Grandma.
"We don't want it
to fall over again."

The sheep was very hungry,
and it started
to eat some grass.
"It's all right now," said Jessica.

The sheep walked away.
Daniel smiled.
"We saved it," he said.
"I saw it
on its back
waving its legs
and we
saved it."